A Gift
from the
Wise Men

**Change Your Thinking
and Make a Difference**

Vince Young

Pittsgrove, New Jersey
2021

Copyright 2021 © Vince Young

All rights reserved

No part of this book may be reproduced, stored or transmitted in any form or by any means, electronic or mechanical, including photocopying, recording or by any information storage and retrieval system, without the written permission of the publisher, except in case of brief quotation embodied in critical articles and reviews.

Book and cover design by Robin Wrighton

ISBN: 978-0-578-98768-2

Young, Vince / A Gift from the Wise Men:
Change Your Thinking and Make a Difference

Published by
Pittsgrove Publishing
www.vinceyoungauthor.com
vyoung1965@gmail.com

Printed in the United States of America

*To my wife Joan
For her support, encouragement
and example throughout our lifetime together.*

Contents

Preface vii

Part I **Introduction**

Chapter 1 The Three Wise Men 1
Chapter 2 Rules of Engagement 7

Part II **Values and Beliefs**

Chapter 3 Alex 15
Chapter 4 Chris 21
Chapter 5 Ben 26
Chapter 6 Examining How We Think 32

Part III **Thinking Differently**

Chapter 7 Religion and Spirituality 41
Chapter 8 Equality 47
Chapter 9 Money 54
Chapter 10 Leadership 60
Chapter 11 The Message 66

Part IV **Possibilities**

Chapter 12 Searching for Perfection 75
Chapter 13 Caring and Sharing 81
Chapter 14 Addressing Poverty 86
Chapter 15 Leadership 92
Chapter 16 Problem Solving 97
Chapter 17 Global Synergy 103

Epilogue 108
Appendix I Problem-Solving Process 113
Appendix II Topics for Discussion 117
Appendix III Selected Readings 121

Preface

This book offers a story about possibilities that can spring from thinking differently. As I finished writing this at the start of 2021 we were still in the grip of a global pandemic, and we were losing many of our loved ones. The pandemic came with a severe emotional and economic burden and kept us apart from our families. We continued to live with racial injustice, gun violence, terrorism and poverty while political turmoil only heightened our concerns. When I looked to the future I saw more of the same and I saw few signs of hope. But hope is what we need most. We must see the possibilities rather than the problems.

Albert Einstein once said, "The problems that exist in the world today cannot be solved by the level of thinking that created them." He was telling us to think differently in order to uncover new possibilities. We can't address our chronic problems by doing the same things that didn't work in the past. We must search for new approaches and that is what this story is about. In order to be able to think differently, we need to first examine our beliefs and values because they help us to understand how we arrived at our present way of thinking. Once we uncover what we believe and how we came to believe it, we will be able to change the way we think. This examination will help us to shift our perspective and allow new possibilities to emerge, thus creating new hope for the future.

My objective for this book is to show how respectful dialogue and the examination of values in a nonjudgmental way can help us to think differently and lead us to a new way of being. The possibilities described here are meant as examples of what could be if we accept that we can't solve problems without changing our thinking. These are only a few of the many possibilities that could result from a thoughtful examination of society's problems by people like you and me, working at a grassroots level, who wish to leave the world a better place for our children. We can start by giving voice to those who are already making a positive difference in the world.

This parable is meant to help you to think differently, bring hope to the future, and show that wisdom can arrive when you least expect it.

PART I

Introduction

Chapter 1

The Three Wise Men

I first encountered the wise men in January 2021. Looking back, I realized that these three appeared at the same time as the biblical wise men did, at what Christians call "Little Christmas" or Epiphany. It was a typical warm and sunny day in Florida, which is why I spend my winters here since I retired. I had come to the park near my condo looking for a place to sit, take in the weather, read a book and reflect on the times we live in. Most people, including myself, had been beaten down by the pandemic and I was feeling lucky that I had only been inconvenienced, while many other people had suffered severe physical, emotional and economic impacts. To compound our national feelings of hopelessness, just the previous week on January 6, an angry mob stormed the Capitol and only added to our ongoing political chaos. Meanwhile, our chronic societal problems persisted. That didn't feel like much of a foundation on which to create hope for a positive New Year.

I found a bench and sat down to read my book, but I had a hard time concentrating. My mind was an endless train of thoughts and questions that I was wrestling with.

What can I do to make a difference?

Can we count on our leaders to act and look for solutions that will be effective and long lasting?

What kind of a society will we leave behind for our children?

It was clear to me that day that we need to change our approach and create some innovative solutions. We need to work together to fix the causes rather than put Band-Aids on the symptoms. Solutions continue to elude us as we spiral downwards without answers to the questions that many of us have been wrestling with. I promised myself that this was the year that I would write my book and look for new ideas to help solve our chronic problems. Maybe it was time to get started.

I soon heard raised voices coming from the benches behind me.

"Don't blame Trump, his power comes from us. We are to blame," said someone in the group behind me.

Another voice responded, "But we have to look to our leaders for help and guidance in times of turmoil."

A third person added, "I agree with Chris, I don't see permanent solutions coming from our political leaders, either. We have to look for different solutions."

Chapter 1 | The Three Wise Men

As the discussion continued, I realized that the voices were passionate, not angry like so many political discussions are these days. The 2020 election season brought out the worst in many of us and it was refreshing to hear people talking about politics in a conversation with no arguing and full of wisdom and obvious respect for one another.

I could not help but listen since the tone was nonconfrontational, with innovative solutions that were shared and listened to by the others. This sounded like a truly unusual group. As they continued sharing ideas, I decided to go over and introduce myself.

"Hi, guys. I'm Vince Young, a snowbird from New Jersey enjoying the weather and I couldn't help overhearing your discussion. I came over to tell you how thought provoking your ideas are. It is difficult these days to find people engaged in respectful conversation about politics without them arguing about the latest conspiracy theory floating around on Facebook. Do you mind if I sit in, at least to listen?"

The Black man in the group looked at me with a bemused smile and said, "That is exactly how I became part of this august group of wise men. I'm sure we will be wiser with you in our group. My name is Ben Davidson and I have been retired for four years. I moved here to escape the winters in Chicago. I live near the park and use it for my daily power walks." That explained why he looked so fit. "One day I was walking by these two and they asked me to enlighten them."

The tall, distinguished, well-dressed man responded, "Yes, it's true that we asked Ben to enlighten us. I asked him where he got that ugly jogging suit." The three men chuckled in the manner of good friends sharing a well-worn joke. "Hi, Vince, I'm Chris Conover. I live in a condo over on the Intercoastal and have been here for twenty-seven years selling real estate. I love seeing the snowbirds. It means the weather is good and the buyers are here! I moved down here from Washington, DC, after my time spent as a senator's aide. My job is to keep an eye on these two so that they don't cause a ruckus and bring down property values in the area."

I glanced over at the other gentleman, and he looked at me with an expression that said, "I don't talk much, but when I do, you'd better be listening." He then broke into a smile, extended his hand and said, "Hi, I'm Alex Middleton. I retired here from Boston where I taught high school."

Alex had thinning white hair and sparkling blue eyes to go with his serious demeanor. Not fat, but thick in the middle, he had strong arms and was dressed in a Florida State sweatshirt, baggy khakis, and white sneakers.

"Please finish your discussion," I said. "Even though I tuned in when you were in the middle,

Chapter 1 | The Three Wise Men

I was impressed by the innovative thinking. I would like to hear your conclusions and I apologize if I caused you to lose momentum."

"That's okay, we usually wrap up about now anyway," said Ben. "We can only take so much of the senator in one day."

Alex added, "You are more than welcome to join us whenever you can, we are usually here Monday, Wednesday and Friday from late morning to early afternoon, if you're interested. We do have some unwritten rules that help to make our discussions more productive, and we can share them with you when we next meet. You won't be fined for violating them, but I think you will find the conversations more enlightening."

I was excited to find this opportunity to express my intellectual enthusiasm with others without falling into endless, ego-driven arguments about maintaining the status quo. Had I discovered a way to boost my outlook on society and create a sense of hope for the future?

As we all prepared to leave, I said, "I have been looking for fuel for a book that I would like to write. It would be about how to find innovative solutions to the chronic problems facing our society and creating an atmosphere of hope for the future. My objective is to examine our beliefs and values, and to practice thinking differently and brainstorming new possibilities. I think that your group has the attitude and insight to create a wealth of ideas that I could include. Would you allow me to record our discussions, take notes and observe? I'd give you the chance to approve anything that I write before I use it in the book."

"No problem," said Chris and Ben.

"Only if you participate with new ideas," said Alex.

I was ecstatic. I'd found willing sources of information for my book, an outlet for my creative thoughts, and hope for the future – all on one trip to the park. I had hit the trifecta!

"Great! Thank you, gentlemen, and I'll see you Monday," I said as I walked away.

Chapter 2

Rules of Engagement

When I got to the park on Monday, I found Alex and Ben already there, drinking coffee and enjoying their surroundings.

"Good morning" I said. "Where's Chris on this bright Monday?"

"He sometimes gets hung up showing a house and may arrive closer to lunchtime," said Alex. "We can get started by sharing our informal rules of engagement with you. Ben will start off, since he introduced many of these rules that have proven so effective."

"Sure. Vince, have you ever heard of Dr. Stephen Covey?"

"Yes. I read his book *The 7 Habits of Highly Effective People* back in 1992. I remember that there were several important principles, and that if we incorporated them into our life, it would make us more effective. I believe it was primarily focused on business people but could be applied in our personal life as well."

"That is true, I had the same impression the first time I read it, but I eventually embraced the principles in my personal life as well as in my work life," said Ben. "As corporate director of human resources for a Fortune 500 company I became a Covey disciple and taught the principles to others several times, with great success. One of those principles is our group's first rule: Seek first to understand, then to be understood."

"Can you refresh my memory on what that means?"

"Normally during a conversation between two people, the listener is collecting his thoughts in order to respond to the speaker," Ben replied. "You are preparing to show empathy, impress with an intelligent response, ask a question for clarity, or disagree. Meanwhile you are only partially listening, which causes you to miss important verbal and physical signals that could be invaluable to the discussion. Dr. Covey says we need to practice listening, which will allow us to be better understood when it is our turn to speak."

"So, the first rule is to listen?"

"Actively listen and seek to understand," Ben emphasized. "This leads us into the second rule, which really is an extension of the first rule. Disagreement with another is not allowed until you can restate the opposing view to the satisfaction of the other person. This demonstrates that we understand exactly what we are disagreeing with. Often, we disagree with another, and it turns out that we didn't completely understand their view,

Chapter 2 | Rules of Engagement

and that when we did understand it our opposition dissipated."

"How will I know when I have violated this rule?"

"Oh, you'll know! We'll be jumping all over you requiring you to listen again, restate the opposing position and reconsider your disagreement." Ben smiled "You may still disagree, but you must show that you understand what you are disagreeing with. This has proven especially useful in our discussions to avoid misunderstandings."

"I can see how this rule can keep discussions from becoming arguments and promote the exchange of information. If everyone would follow this rule, there would be fewer confrontations in our society."

"I agree, my experience taught me that it makes for effective listening and leads to questions calling for clarification," said Ben. "I am also responsible for the third rule, which is to work on the cause of a problem and not the symptoms. As a management trainee working for a manufacturing company, I had to spend some time in the manufacturing departments where I was exposed to many problem-solving techniques, especially in the Quality Control Department. They were always focused on searching for the root cause of problems, so that they were applying their efforts to fixing the cause rather than relieving the symptoms. A manager once told me that if you fix the cause, the symptoms will take care of themselves, and we have found that advice to be particularly useful."

Puzzled, I asked, "Can you give me an example to help me understand?"

"Sure. One day you come home from work, and you find a puddle of water on your new hardwood floor and there is a slow drip coming from the ceiling. You mop the floor and put a trashcan under the drip to prevent any more water from collecting on the new floor. You pronounce the problem solved, but have you really solved the problem or just addressed the symptom?"

"I see the point. The problem still exists, so more analysis needs to be done to find the cause, even though the threat to the floor is taken care of."

"Precisely, a little more analysis would tell you that since the drip is located under the upstairs bathroom, something may be leaking up there. A little detective work and a pipe wrench should solve the root cause of the problem."

Just then Chris arrived, looking dapper in a golf shirt, pressed khakis and polished loafers, as if he had spent the morning on the golf course rather than showing houses.

"Good afternoon," he said. "Sorry I'm a little late, this darn job keeps getting in the way of my free time. What are you guys talking about?"

Alex said, "Ben just went over the listening and problem-solving rules, and I was about to

Chapter 2 | Rules of Engagement

add some others. Vince, it's impossible to create new possibilities as a group without mutual respect throughout the entire team. From day one of our conversations with each other, we have always respected each other's opinions and life experiences. You will find that we are all different. But those differences enrich our discussions. From the short time that I have known you, I suspect that you agree."

"Absolutely! That was one of the reasons I asked to join," I replied. "I could sense the mutual respect among you when I was eavesdropping on Friday. It was so unlike the typical arguments that I hear all around me."

"Great! We also encourage everyone to share their intelligence but not their bias. There is no place for judgements in our circle, so please leave your ego at home. Be kind and you will fit right in. Chris, do you have anything to add?"

"Yes, I do. Vince, we consider ourselves to be innovative thinkers, but we would never accomplish that if we discarded new ideas as unworthy of discussion; there are no dumb ideas that can't be improved with open, honest discussion. With these rules in place, and people willing to think differently, I think we can make your book worthwhile for your readers."

"Speaking of your book, Vince," said Alex. "Have you thought about an organized approach to our discussions that will flow into your book?"

"I have done some planning, but I don't want to get ahead of the spontaneous flow of your discussions. Since you are each unique, I suspect that you all have different values, beliefs and characteristics that form the foundation of who you are and what you think. I would like to begin with a conversation about your values and beliefs and how they influence you today. Understanding what makes us think the way we do will make it easier to open our minds to a new perspective."

Alex concurred, "That seems to be a logical place to start."

Ben and Chris agreed enthusiastically.

We agreed on Friday for our next discussion and headed our separate ways.

As I walked home through the park, I was excited. I sensed that my life and perceptions of society were about to change. I felt that people like the wise men working within a structure like the one they described could uncover many possibilities for our future.

PART II

Values and Beliefs

Chapter 3

Alex

I woke up that Friday morning with some nagging questions in my mind about our upcoming conversation.

Would relative strangers be open about their values?

Would anything productive come of our discussions?

Had I overestimated the knowledge of these three senior gentlemen?

Could there possibly be new ideas coming from this group or would it be just old, tired ideas from the past?

I had been so excited when I left the park on Monday that maybe I had placed too much hope on simple conversations, although I was impressed by the structure that they followed in their discussions. I decided I would be patient and allow the discussions to go where they took us.

My enthusiasm picked up as I arrived in the park, and I saw the wise men already actively engaged in conversation. They were energetic and excited about our project and eager to get started.

A Gift from the Wise Men

"Welcome to the house of the wise men," said Chris as I sat down. "You have arrived at the place of enlightenment, so bring us your readers and we'll give them the gift of our wisdom."

The others rolled their eyes and Alex suggested we get started since he had been thinking a lot since our last discussion, and his self-examination had generated some new insights that he was anxious to share.

"Why don't you start us off, Alex?" I said. "But let me get my recorder set and then we can begin."

Alex then began his story. "Back in 2002 I had an epiphany that changed how I looked at life and the beliefs and values that made me who I am. You know that I was a teacher for my whole career, but for the first eighteen years I was a Catholic priest and taught religion in a boy's high school in Boston. I had been raised in a Catholic home where my parents and I went to church every Sunday and faithfully followed the teachings of the Church. In early 2002, *The Boston Globe* published an exposé on the sexual abuse of minors by priests in Boston. Bishops were complicit for transferring abusers to different parishes to cover up the scandal and the abuse was eventually found to be a worldwide problem throughout the Church."

"I was devastated," Alex continued quietly. "My entire foundation of faith was shattered. My values were compromised, and I was lost. I soon

Chapter 3 | Alex

decided to leave the priesthood because I couldn't continue to be part of what was taking place. I realized the danger in that path, since many people would assume I was involved if I suddenly left the priesthood; but I couldn't stay and be part of it."

"This crisis of faith led me on a spiritual journey that caused me to reexamine my beliefs; a reexamination that has left me in a better spiritual place than where I was in 2002," Alex said. "This journey consisted of meditation, where I quieted my mind and received guidance from God and from experiences and intersections along the way. These intersections were places where I was influenced by the words or actions of others. At these intersections I encountered a number of authors and people who cared for others and demonstrated spiritual love."

"Can you elaborate on the experiences and intersections that influenced you during your journey?" I asked.

"One of the intersections that helped me to understand this new perspective was Neil Donald Walsch in his book *God's Message to the World*. This book gave me a new perspective on teachings that I had followed my whole life. I had never thought to question why God would make us imperfect, give us free will and then threaten us with hell if we used it the wrong way. I never questioned why the commandments were a list of *what not to do,* rather than a list of *what to do.* I never wondered why God didn't keep talking with us after delivering the Bible to us. We were to follow the rules handed down 2000 years ago that have been recorded and revised over that time by imperfect humans. I taught and followed these rules without question until I lost my faith in the church and opened my mind to a more loving scenario; one that wasn't dominated by fear, punishment and rules."

Alex added, "My spiritual journey has led me to a new understanding of who we are. We are not our bodies; we are our soul. We all have a part of God within us that is our perfect essence. We are all equal and this affects how I see others. I don't see people in categories, I see them as equals. Our infinite soul observes humanity through the experiences of many different imperfect, finite bodies over the course of the soul's journey. Our soul is perfect, is already in heaven and is experiencing humanity in order to understand what it is not. God does not decide what is good and evil in the human world, humans do. He is not a judge of our behavior, humans are. God is simply a witness of our human imperfection."

Alex noted that he also found inspiration from Deepak Chopra and his law of dynamic exchange, which he presents in his book *The Seven Spiritual Laws of Success.* Chopra outlines "The Law of Giving" that teaches us that if we want

Chapter 3 | Alex

the flow of something coming to us, we need to first give it away. "If we want money, be generous," said Alex. "If we want love, love others, if we want peace of mind, then help somebody else to achieve it. Marianne Williamson, in her book *A Return to Love,* helped me to see the power of love in changing the world. In *Many Lives Many Masters,* Brian Weiss taught me to understand meditation and how to use it to listen to God. Keeping an open mind, slowing at intersections, and shedding my old way of thinking all helped me to find new beliefs that give me the freedom to explore my spirituality rather than following rules to earn a reward sometime in the future."

"How long does a transformation like this take?" asked Ben.

"It continues today," Alex replied. "The pieces are continuing to click into place with new circumstances and events in my life. When a new thought comes to me, I ask myself if that makes sense, considering my beliefs. That is something I never could do in the Church. Questions weren't encouraged if they didn't support the rules. I was not encouraged to explore my spirituality outside of the teachings."

Chris added, "I am fascinated by the concept that everyone is perfect inside but to see their perfection we have to see through the human shell. Some people are hard to visualize as perfect with the antics of their humanity on display. How do you deal with that?"

"It's not easy with some people, but that is the challenge, and it requires patience and forgiveness," said Alex. "Remember that you are perfect too, practice seeing your own perfection instead of your shortcomings. That will help you to find it in others."

I was curious about meditation and how it worked, and I asked Alex, "What is the difference between meditation and prayer? Aren't they similar?"

"Not really. Prayer usually involves a request of some kind where you ask for help, support, or a change in circumstances. You go into the state of prayer with what you feel is the outcome that is best. Meditation is an exercise in quieting your mind and listening for guidance. The outcome may be different than what you had planned but it is from a divine source that is perfect. The guidance may take you in a different, more productive direction then you could've imagined on your own, and it may take some time, but an open mind and patience will be rewarded."

"Thank you, Alex, I can see how your journey has been enlightening and transformational for you. I clearly see how your experiences and intersections have influenced how you think; it has already got me thinking in a new way. Chris, would you like to discuss your values and beliefs and how they help you to react to events?"

Chapter 4

Chris

Chris began, "That was an inspiring story, Alex. Finding yourself in a better place after a shattering experience speaks volumes about your character and values. This holds special significance for me because I also had a watershed experience that negatively affected my beliefs and values as I was beginning my career."

"I was raised in a mid-sized city in the Midwest and my father was highly active in local government," Chris recalled. "He eventually was elected mayor with an eye on state representative when he died of a heart attack. I was always interested in the political process, and we would have long talks about the role of elected officials, their role as leaders and their duty to assure that everyone was treated fairly and with equal respect. He was my hero and I wanted to be like him. I even ran for class president in high school but lost in a landslide to the captain of the football team."

"When I went on to college, I majored in political science with hopes of going on to law school and eventually into politics," he continued.

"During my senior year I was given the opportunity to work as a senator's aide for two years in Washington. I was willing to delay law school for the opportunity to learn about politics at the highest level and see our government leaders at work. My dad would've been proud. I immersed myself in the environment. I was loaded down with research work and other administrative tasks for the senator, but I was excited about being right in the middle of the government at work. I saw the results of my work showing up in proposed legislation, which gave me some insight into how legislation was created. I occasionally saw the explosion of egos and party squabbling but shook that off as petty politics. These were our leaders fighting for their constituents' rights in Washington."

"Over the course of the first year, I started to see through my naiveté," Chris admitted. "I began to see too much legislation that was prompted by lobbyists rather than the needs of constituents. I saw new members of Congress arrive wide-eyed and committed, like me, hoping to make a difference, only to find that they had to change their values, or they would find no support at reelection time. I saw too many instances where politicians abandoned some of the people they served, in order to serve special interests that provided money to the party. I saw arm-twisting and veiled threats from the party to toe the line if

Chapter 4 | Chris

they wanted reelection support. Where was the leadership and respect for others? It was all about money, ego and the party line. I saw times when some classes of people were treated differently from others. When I ended my first year, I considered getting out, but I had made a commitment and my dad always taught me to honor my word, so I stayed, hoping for improvement."

"During the second year my initial enthusiasm had worn completely off, and I saw politics for what it was," said Chris. "I saw firsthand how money from special interests influenced decisions and legislation. I saw how the needs of constituents were met only to secure votes for reelection. Leadership was replaced with loyalty to the party. It was political suicide to voice your beliefs if they didn't support the party. I realized that there was no similarity between the politics of my dad and the politics of Washington. All in all, I'd say my experience with values and beliefs was different from Alex's."

"What do you mean?" I asked.

"Alex's crisis of faith provided an opportunity to examine and expand his beliefs," Chris replied. "He questioned the values and characteristics that he followed his whole life and was able to arrive at a new understanding that has 'left him in a better spiritual place,' to use his words. I'm sure that discarding old, long-held beliefs and enhancing them was a difficult journey for him, but it led to a new and more satisfying belief system. My values came face-to-face with the opposite as displayed in the Washington political environment, and that left me feeling hopeless."

"Where I believe in equality and fairness for all, they believe in responding to the flow of money.

Where I believe in serving constituents equally, they believe in ego.

Where I believe in leadership and pursuing the common good, they believe in following the party line.

Where I believe in finding innovative solutions, they believe in the status quo.

At the end of my two years, I was dispirited and left politics behind. Over the last twenty-seven years I have watched Washington politics continue to deteriorate into hateful dialogue, confrontation between parties and ineffective problem solving."

Alex said, "That must have been difficult for you, Chris, but when you started your story, you said this had a negative effect on your values, but your values haven't changed. Your values are clear and strong and grounded by your upbringing. If anything, they have solidified. I'm sure that you met some politicians who felt like you, whose hands were tied by the political process. They, like you, are faced with a challenge because their values are different from the status quo. Your examination

Chapter 4 | Chris

has reaffirmed your beliefs and provided you with an opportunity to make a difference for others. Maybe we can find some possibilities in the course of our discussions."

"Thank you, Alex, I never really looked at it that way before," said Chris thoughtfully. "But you're right, all I see is the difference between them and me. What I need to examine is how we can be brought closer together and help them to find the motivation to change. I must remember to look for the perfection in them and search for appropriate solutions. That is a big help to me."

I added, "Reexamining what we believe and its effect on us can lead us to unexpected places and prompt solutions where none seemed possible before. So far, we've had one examination that led to an enhancement of beliefs and one that reinforced long-held beliefs. Both have led to some different thinking for all of us. Ben, how were your values shaped and how have they affected your life experiences?"

Chapter 5

Ben

"I also had an experience when I was only a teenager that caused me to examine what is important to me and prompts my response to events around me, or what we are calling beliefs and values," said Ben. "I grew up on the streets of Chicago in the mid-sixties. Gangs controlled the neighborhoods and defended their turf from rival gangs. Boys and young men armed with guns, knives and egos ruled the streets. My brother, who was three years older than me, was active in a local gang and was grooming me to join him. I was only 15, but I was eager to become a gang member, because 'street cred' was the value that we lived by."

"When my brother was killed in a meaningless turf war, my life was turned upside down. His gang was telling me that I had to stand up and defend my brother's honor by joining the gang in his place. My parents were at a loss on how to change my mind. They couldn't cope with losing another son to the streets."

"At the funeral, I was glad to see my Uncle Joe," Ben recalled. "We've always been close. He

Chapter 5 | Ben

lives in a town outside of Chicago where there are trees and lakes and baseball fields. When I was a child, I would spend summers with him and we would swim, toss a ball and explore together. We started to talk about my brother, and I told him that I had been asked to join the gang in his place and I was trying to decide what to do. He looked at me with a sad expression and said, 'Close your eyes and get a mental picture of yourself at age thirty – if you're still alive. What do you look like? Are you a respectable man with a family or are you a punk? Whichever one you see is how you should live your life at 15."

Ben continued, "I finally saw what everyone had been telling me. After a short discussion with my parents, my uncle invited me to come live with him and said that he would help me get through high school and into college. I just had to supply the hard work. From that day on, my values began to change. My new environment helped me to see life differently and my dreams took flight. I didn't want to be a punk. I did well in school and earned a scholarship to Northwestern's prestigious business school."

"This childhood experience taught me the value of love, how ego can get in the way and that we are more powerful when we don't try to do it alone," Ben concluded. "I realized that I was looking at the world through the eyes of a gang member and there are other ways to see the world."

At this point, Chris observed, "What a powerful story! You were truly on the edge of disaster and without the kindness of your uncle you probably wouldn't be here sharing this story with us. But first you had to see things differently. Wasn't that difficult for a 15-year-old boy who grew up on the streets?"

"Very," Ben replied. "My summers with Uncle Joe had opened my eyes to another world; I just didn't realize that it was attainable for me. Uncle Joe taught me about love, helping one another, and the power of working together. This insight helped to set the direction for my studies at Northwestern and my career choice. I wanted to be in a position where I could help others the way that I was helped at a critical time in my life. I chose to major in Human Resources Management and when I started my career, I took a job in that area of specialization."

"I realized I had made the right choice when I was first assigned to the training department," said Ben. "This group was responsible for researching training needs throughout the organization, finding the appropriate material and delivering the training to employees. It was rewarding because it was necessary to search out who needed help, find the appropriate resources, and then put them in use to help them, much like what Uncle Joe did for me."

"My career provided me with the opportunity to learn problem-solving techniques like team building, root cause analysis and how to find innovative solutions to long-standing problems. This is when I discovered the work of Dr. Covey that I mentioned earlier in our discussion of rules. His books are full of wisdom and to this day help me to develop what he calls a moral compass, or values and beliefs. Covey teaches that our moral compass provides direction for our life. This direction is called true north and doesn't change when the map changes. We are always headed for true north, even when life takes us in a different direction temporarily. Our life experiences are the lens through which we see the world around us. Everyone has different experiences, so the view is different for each of us, and creates our perspective. Our perspective can change with different experiences and an open mind."

"Which of the seven habits do you think is the most important?" Alex asked.

"That depends on the person," Ben answered. "The habits are designed for making us more effective as individuals as well as when interacting with others. You may find one or two more appropriate for you based on your own shortcomings, but one that has helped me a great deal is what he refers to as 'synergize.' Covey says that the other habits, when used interactively, will create synergy. He refers to synergy as 'the essence of value-driven leadership' and it means that the sum is greater than its parts added together.

Synergy occurs when the efforts of a group of people working separately are less effective than groups of people working together. This is the basic belief behind problem-solving teams."

"You mean like we use here in the park?" I asked.

"Exactly," said Ben. "We have effective discussions here because we put aside our egos, share mutual respect, and have different perspectives and life experiences. They allow us to synergize and demonstrate our power as a group. A power from within is more effective and more durable than power that comes from outside us."

"Can you give me an example?" I asked.

"The power for the gang came from their guns, violence and threats. If you take these away, they have no power. Uncle Joe's power, love and respect, came from within himself and can't be taken away."

"So, our values and love for one another can be more powerful than inflated status or wealth," I said. "What we are is more significant than what we have. I get it. That was a stimulating conversation. I think it was worth the time we spent on it, and I learned so much from your experiences and insights. Now we can use what we have learned from each other to help us to open our minds. Let's meet on Wednesday to discuss how our values and beliefs shape the way we think, since we can't think differently without

Chapter 5 | Ben

examining what makes us think the way we do. I'll see you then."

As everyone departed, I couldn't help but think about how apprehensive I had been this morning before we started. I couldn't be happier about how the day went, and I was anxious to continue our journey together.

Chapter 6

Examining How We Think

When Wednesday arrived, I found that I was full of enthusiasm, unlike Friday when I let my apprehension affect my outlook. On another gorgeous day I took the short walk to the park, and I was the first to arrive, so I sat and enjoyed the day while I reviewed my notes. Soon Ben arrived from his power walk, a little out of breath.

"Good morning," he said. "I think I'm getting too old for this; it may be time to retire my walking shoes and spend more time relaxing."

"Looking at your fitness level, I don't believe you," I said. "You look like you have taken care of yourself all of your life."

"Actually, Covey's seventh habit is to 'sharpen the saw.' The principle is to renew the four dimensions of our nature – physical, spiritual, mental and social/emotional, and I try to attend to them all and keep them in balance in order to be more effective. These discussions help in all four dimensions."

"Covey has certainly influenced you throughout your life," I said and made a mental note to reread *The 7 Habits of Highly Effective People*.

Chapter 6 | Examining How We Think

Chris and Alex arrived, and we exchanged pleasantries and settled in, while I started the recorder.

I began, "In our discussion on values and beliefs, the three of you presented examples of how a reexamination of your beliefs led you to a better understanding of yourself. Your stories were life changing and were triggered by some type of emotional event, and in Alex's and Ben's case, left them with new beliefs and values. In Chris's case, he reinforced what he already believed, but in all three cases the reexamination provided new perspective and allowed you to change your life for the better. All of you encountered a situation where your original beliefs came from someplace outside of you, either the teachings of the Church, the gang or your father. After your reexamination, you owned your beliefs. They were yours and you could live by them."

Chris said, "Maybe I should have done something over the last 27 years to change what I considered to be wrong, rather than quit and do nothing. Alex and Ben changed themselves with new beliefs."

"We're discussing values here not action plans," Alex responded. "We changed our beliefs and values; you didn't find things to change. Because someone else lacks your values doesn't make yours wrong or require action by you."

"That's true, but I feel that I have never questioned my values or truly examined them because I thought they were right," said Chris.

"We all do. Unless something happens to shake our belief, we don't really see the need to re-examine them. One thing I have learned in my journey of understanding is that there was a lot that I didn't know. Opening my mind to what others thought gave me a new perspective and helped me to question my beliefs. First you must expose yourself to different ideas and then absorb them with an open mind. You may eventually discard them, but you also may find some morsels of truth. Over time you may see an evolution of your beliefs that may be different or just an enhanced understanding of what you believe."

"That is the true meaning of reexamination," I said. "Once you look deeply at something you may see it differently than you did before. Most importantly, it allows you to look at old problems in a new way, which is what we are trying to do here."

Alex continued, "I mentioned previously that on my spiritual journey I have learned that we all are perfect within an imperfect body. That perfection within us offers us perfect wisdom but must pass through an imperfect human filter: us. That filter distorts the message, but some of the perfection gets through. We need to realize that there may be some perfect wisdom in what we say and experience from others and consider it wisely."

"So, to sum up your experience; in lieu of an epiphany, you can proactively examine your beliefs by exposing yourself to new ideas, keeping an open mind, and looking for the perfection in yourself and others," I said.

"Precisely," said Alex. "And don't judge others on their human behavior."

Ben said, "We are heavily influenced by tradition and status quo. My brother's gang had traditions, rituals and rules that kept them from exploring different beliefs. They never questioned them because they were happy with the status quo. An open mind is important but can be hard to achieve. Our perspective is developed over the course of our life and is the lens through which we see the world. We make assessments of others that can be completely wrong and sometimes ignore other possibilities because they don't fit our assumptions."

"Let me tell you a story about a perspective that was changed in a split second and taught me to reexamine previous assumptions about people and events," Ben continued. "When I traveled for business, I would kill time in the airport by watching people, and by studying them, I would try to determine something about them. On one trip I was putting my briefcase in the overhead bin when my seatmate arrived and removed his coat. I noticed that he was wearing the most hideous tie and shirt that I had ever seen. Nice shoes and suit, but the shirt and tie told me that he got dressed in a dark closet. On some planet you could almost say they went together; some subtle colors were from the same family, but I'm talking tiny fruits and vegetables adorning the tie and a multicolored striped shirt."

"I wanted to see if I could predict some things about him based on his wardrobe," Ben went on. "We were headed to New York, so he wasn't a farmer who never got dressed up. So I figured he was probably an engineer of some type without any fashion sense. I decided to test my perception and struck up a conversation with him. I introduced myself and eventually we started to talk about our business lives. When I asked him what line of business he was in, he told me he was the founder of a men's fashion house in New York City."

"I was flabbergasted. I'm thinking is it 'The Bozo the Clown Fashion Emporium'? How could I be so wrong? But I couldn't resist asking if that shirt and tie was from his collection. 'Oh this,' the man said, indicating his shirt and tie, 'my wife gave them to me for my birthday before she died, and I wear them every year on my birthday to honor her sense of humor.' I learned a lesson that day about judging others from appearances. Making assumptions based on prior experiences can make you look foolish."

"Thank you all for your insights," I said. "I believe that you have established the importance of questioning our beliefs, recognizing where they come from and how they affect our way of

Chapter 6 | Examining How We Think

thinking. I would like to turn now to some discussion on thinking differently. In order to create innovative solutions, I feel that we need to discuss issues that have either kept us from finding solutions to our chronic societal problems or have contributed to them. By analyzing them with an open mind we may be able to eliminate some obstacles to problem solving. For our next session, let's bring examples of how we can think differently, or topics that present obstacles to the creation of new and innovative possibilities for the future. In other words, a way of thinking that gets in the way of solutions. See you on Friday."

PART III

Thinking Differently

Chapter 7

Religion and Spirituality

I had spent the previous day preparing some topics to prompt some interesting discussions to get us started on Friday, but I hoped that my wise men would bring some as well. We needed to get outside of the box and create some examples of thinking in a new way.

"A little chilly today," said Ben as he approached our benches, "but nowhere near what it is in Chicago today. I can live with this." Just then Alex and Chris arrived with coffee and bagels, and we all settled down for a lively discussion.

I began by asking, "Does anyone have any topics to inspire us to think differently?"

Chris jumped in immediately. "I think that we need some new thinking around the subject of equality. Given the continued racial injustice that we see all around us, it seems that we need some new thinking. Our present approach does not appear to be effective."

"Naturally, I agree," Ben said, "but sometime in the next few sessions we also need to look at the effect that the pursuit of money has on our society. Money is at the heart of many of our problems and needs some discussion."

"Great topics that I can't wait to sink my teeth into!" said Alex. "I thought that a discussion around our spirituality and how it is viewed could open our minds, because most everyone has strong views about spirituality and religion."

"I like the sound of that to start us off," said Chris. "Let's start there, if there are no objections."

"Let's go," I said.

"What is the difference between spirituality and religion?" Alex began.

Everyone looked thoughtful for a moment and then Chris spoke up. "Isn't spirituality where you find God on your own and religion is where you follow an organized approach?"

"Yes, that's a good description," Alex said. "Most people believe that our life is a pursuit of heaven and that by participating in a certain religion we can stay on track by following rules, performing rituals, and avoiding evil. But many people, like me, still believe in God but find that organized religion is not the only way to reach Him. When I left the priesthood, I was confronted with finding my spirituality without the support of organized religion."

"I guess that time was difficult for you, Alex, but I'm sure that you learned to think differently," I said.

Chapter 7 | Religion and Spirituality

"Yes, it was. I felt like a man without a home and that is when I began my spiritual journey of understanding that led me to my beliefs. I have an image in my mind of how spirituality and religion are both similar and different, which may help you to visualize my description of spirituality."

Alex continued, "Picture a large circle that represents a forest, and in the center of the forest is a small clearing, which is where God exists, or what I will call heaven. Our spiritual mission is to move from the outer perimeter, through the forest and reach heaven. Remember, my belief is that the body takes the journey with our soul as a witness. The soul is learning from our experiences and is already in heaven. The body is finite and judged only by other humans. Now, picture several paths cut through the forest that travel directly from the starting place on the perimeter directly to God. These superhighways represent the various organized religions and have guardrails, or rules, to keep you from going astray."

"So, these highways are the fast track to God, and help you avoid wandering through the forest looking for God. Why wouldn't you take this road?" I asked.

"Pierre Teilhard de Chardin said it best," replied Alex. "'We are not human beings having a spiritual experience, but spiritual beings having a human experience.' The journey is for the soul to learn what it is not, so human experiences are part of the journey. The fast track provides less learning with its rules and guardrails. Experiencing spirituality without the limitations imposed by organized religion can lead to expanded learning. The soul must have a broad range of experiences in order to complete its mission, so the winding path through the forest of spirituality is different from the guarded highways. There will be many more questions and more learning taking place, which will lead to experiences for the soul."

"So, the perfect soul, which is already in heaven, travels with a series of bodies in order to experience humanity," Chris said. "If the soul is perfect, why does it have to experience human imperfection?"

"Neal Donald Walsch says that we cannot experience what we are, in the absence of what we are not," Alex replied. "We cannot know black without understanding white. We cannot experience dry without being wet and the same is true of perfection. God cannot experience perfection in the spiritual realm alone. He must go into other imperfect realms to know what He is not and to understand the challenges that we face."

I said, "I need to be sure that I understand. Religion is based on rules written and revised by humans over many years and celebrated with rituals. Many religions include threats and promises about breaking the rules and some include penalties that can last forever. There is an organization behind them that is led by imperfect humans trying to help us to find God in our lives and many people embrace their religion and find great comfort in it. Spirituality has no rules or organization and requires us to pursue learning and revelation. You admitted, Alex, that your journey has been difficult, so don't you think that people will find it more difficult to reach God this way?"

"This discussion is an exercise in learning to think differently," he said. "I have experienced great joy through my spiritual journey, and I think that by opening our minds we can find something that we did not expect. In a spiritual world we find forgiveness, patience and hope rather than fear, punishment and judgment. We experience universal love and respect by searching for the perfection that lies within us all."

"Thank you, Alex. That discussion opened my mind and helps me to understand that many organized religions and spiritual individuals are all headed in the same direction; they are just following different paths. Like you said, this is an exercise in a new way of thinking that requires time and patience, and it starts by opening our minds. Are there any other thoughts on this topic before moving on?"

Ben commented, "We may want to circle back to some of these discussions to revisit some of these points. My perspective is growing with each discussion, and we might have more to add."

"I'll make a note to do that at the end of this section. How about if we plan our next discussion around Chris's topic on thinking differently about equality? Have a great weekend."

Chapter 8

Equality

When I got to the park on Monday morning, I found Chris already there and he was pacing up and down, deep in thought with a serious expression on his face. His brain was obviously working overtime because he didn't even notice my arrival and I startled him when I said, "Good morning, Chris. I see smoke coming out of your ears, what's cooking?"

"Good morning, Vince. I've just spent a good part of the weekend thinking about equality and I've got a million thoughts running through my head. I'm anxious to share them with the group."

By the time I got my recorder set up, Alex and Ben had arrived, and I suggested we get started before Chris's head exploded.

I began, "Our agreement was to discuss thinking differently about equality, and Chris has spent a good deal of time on it, so the floor is yours, Chris."

"Thank you, Vince. When I left Washington politics, one of the things that influenced my decision was that some people were treated unfairly by our government, even though our country was founded on the principle that 'all men are created equal' and are 'entitled to life, liberty and the pursuit of happiness.' It seems that we, as a country, have always struggled with the meaning of 'equality.' Let me ask, how do you define it?"

Ben replied, "Equality is where everyone is respected and treated the same."

"Equality is where we see the perfection in each other and share our love for one another," said Alex.

"Define everyone," said Chris.

Ben quickly said, "All men, women and children."

"Of any race, religion and sexual preference," added Alex.

"What do you mean, Ben, when you say, 'treated the same'?"

"I mean access to resources and knowledge," answered Ben.

"I noticed that you did not mention illegal immigrants, convicts, predators or residents from foreign countries," said Chris. "Are you including them?"

Ben shook his head with a tentative yes and Alex did not respond.

Chris continued, "This weekend I asked myself the same questions and had similar answers. Equality is hard to define and deciding who it refers to is difficult and inconsistent. Does it mean

Chapter 8 | Equality

showing respect or sharing resources? Does it just apply to our country or is it global? Are 'bad' people excluded? I did a lot of soul searching this weekend after our discussion on spirituality and I realized that Alex's comment regarding seeking perfection in each other seems to be the pathway to equality. We place everyone into categories based on their human condition and make judgements about individuals based on our view of their category. We need to love one another regardless of our shell and behaviors. Love will allow us to see through human behaviors, appearances and circumstances, and embrace the fact that we are equal because we all are made up of a perfect essence. I am not proposing that we overlook bad behaviors that need to be corrected, but I am proposing patience and forgiveness and rehabilitation."

"How do you see this playing out?" asked Alex.

"Looking at the potential results of thinking differently is not our objective here," Chris replied. "The social problems that result from discrimination and injustice are so huge that we would be naïve to think that four senior citizens sitting in the park had all the answers. We are simply trying to take the first step by changing how we think. Love as a response to inequality will require a different way of thinking and provide us with an opportunity to open our minds and see equality through a new lens. We need to find the underlying causes so that we are attacking the right ones when we eventually design our action plans."

Ben said, "My experiences with problem-solving teams have taught me to focus on the opposite of the problem. In this case, how can we become a society where people love one another? What is the opposite of that?"

"How do we eliminate hate?" Alex proposed.

"Exactly!" said Chris.

"Throughout my spiritual journey," said Alex, "I have studied hate and observed how pervasive it can be. We see long-term, deep-seated hate for other races, religions and cultures and we also see short-term, anonymous hate on our roadways. We see hate displayed on social media where it can be posted, absorbed and responded to in an instant, driving us into our bunkers of hate. I've learned to observe hate all around me to learn how to eliminate it."

"How does being aware of it all around you help to eliminate it?" asked Ben.

"Once we become aware of the hate, we begin to realize where it comes from," Alex replied. "It can be triggered by ego when someone attacks your view or can be long-held racism passed down through your family. Hate can take many forms, including words, silence, aggressive behavior or even the withholding of love. As an observer you can be open-minded and that will

Chapter 8 | Equality

allow you to see it where you didn't before. You may observe hate that you carry around that you were not aware of. Consciously observing it in our life will help us to see where it comes from and help us to find ways to eliminate it in our world. Seeing hate can help you to remove it from your own heart."

"So, understanding the causes of hate, and eliminating it, will provide space in your heart for love," said Ben. "But how do we spread the notion to love each other when there are so many groups hating one other?"

Chris responded enthusiastically, "By being aware of how we categorize each other!"

"What do you mean?" I asked.

"Our tendency is to place people into categories so that we can label them, judge them and make assumptions about them based on their category," said Chris. "We all fall into at least one category such as Black, Muslim, female, gay, Baby Boomer or soccer mom. Pick all that fit. It streamlines the process of hate to treat everyone in a category the same way. To find new possibilities in the future, we must avoid categorization and see everyone as equal."

"So, what do we do?" I asked.

As Chris responded, his cheeks flushed with emotion and his voice grew louder. "Think differently about categorization! Once you see the impact of categorization you begin to see racism and discrimination in a different light. Those who have some level of hate for a particular category will not change when they see protests. A demonstration such as Black Lives Matter or Gay Pride only increases the hate in haters and continues to reinforce the categorization of people. The demonstration should be emphasizing the equality of everyone and tearing down the barriers and differences between categories. Banners should proclaim 'There Are No Differences' instead of 'My Category Matters.' Promoting your category only accentuates that there are differences. We need to be blind to the differences. That is how we should think about equality and eventually we will be able to see through the injustice and find equality."

Ben said, "But the injustice is real. I've felt it myself. There are too many instances where Black men are targeted just because they are Black, which too often turns into innocent people being killed."

Chris responded, "I do not take lightly the history of inequality – the history is real. But we are trying to change the thinking that got us here. That is why we must think in a new way. We need to live in a world without categories."

"What an eye-opening discussion," I said. "That has really given me a new perspective, Eliminating categorization instead of reinforcing the differences between categories is a unique way

Chapter 8 | Equality

to look at equality. Seeing the perfection in each other will help us to dull the barriers between groups and cultures and lead to thinking of everyone the same way. If nobody has anything else, then let's meet on Wednesday and we can discuss Ben's topic, the impact of money in our society. See you then."

Chapter 9

Money

On Wednesday everyone arrived eager to start. I felt we were all stimulated by the discussions and looking forward to this one, about money and its influence on us.

"Ben, I thought that you might show up with a whiteboard and PowerPoint presentation," said Chris. "I know that you corporate guys love your graphs, so I was planning to be here until nightfall, but I see that you only brought a notebook."

"There will be a short quiz at the end, so pay attention," Ben quipped.

I said, "Our third topic on thinking differently is money and its influence on our society. So, I'll turn it over to Ben."

"It is my opinion from experiences and observations that money can be found at the root of many of our chronic problems in society. Our world is driven by money, and we are defined and categorized by how much money we have. It seems to be the only measure of success, and the more money we have the greater our celebrity status. Our economy operates on the movement of money from one pocket to another and is unevenly distributed. Money drives our leadership as well as our media and business organizations. Religious and educational institutions can only accomplish their goals by raising money, so, a great amount of their effort goes into fundraising. While all this money is changing hands, some of our children are dying from malnutrition and insufficient living conditions. I believe that we need to find ways to think differently about money and then search for new possibilities."

Chris spoke up. "That's true. We spend more time pursuing wealth than we do on anything else. I saw its influence when I was in Washington. Let's brainstorm some new ways of thinking about money and its influence."

Alex said, "I think we have to look at our attitudes toward money as well as its importance to us."

"What do you mean by attitude?" I asked.

"What I mean is, do you see the world's resources with an abundance mentality, where there is enough to go around; or do you see it with a scarcity mentality, where there isn't enough for everyone? Abundance thinking usually leads to sharing and scarcity thinking leads to hoarding."

"Well, it seems that we are in scarcity mode since there isn't enough to eliminate poverty in the world," Chris said.

"Is that because there aren't enough resources or because of hoarding and uneven distribution of those resources?" Alex responded. "There is no question that there is enough to avoid children starving while others buy luxury items. We need new ways of thinking that will help money make its way to those in need."

"Good point, Alex, but how can we open our minds and wallets to share our abundance?" I pressed.

"Remember what Deepak Chopra said about dynamic exchange, which allows abundance to flow; or in other words; you get what you give away. If you want money, be generous. If you want love, give it away. We must keep the flow of abundance moving or it will die. This spiritual law assures us that if we share our abundance with those in need, then what we want will continue to flow to us."

"That's an excellent example of helping us to think differently, Alex," said Ben. "I have another question: What if money was not the only measure of wealth? What other characteristics could label you as wealthy in the eyes of others? How about happiness? What if one day you released a genie and he granted you one wish, happiness or money? Which would you choose?"

"I see where you are going, Ben," said Chris. "Wealth could be measured with happiness as one of the factors. You would still be considered wealthy if you had a little less money, but you were also happy."

Chapter 9 | Money

"In human resources I've seen it come in to play in many ways," Ben added. "Happiness as a motivator has been overlooked. Every day, people leave lucrative jobs because they are unhappy with the environment or wish to be closer to their family. They choose happiness over money. In the pandemic we see countless examples of people who have dedicated themselves to helping others even though it was threatening to them; choosing to help others, not just for money, but because helping others will bring them happiness. This should be added to their measure of wealth."

"Are there any other characteristics that could help us to measure wealth?"

Ben replied, "Generosity and sharing with others should be a factor; this could motivate people to share excess resources and create a world of abundance for everyone through dynamic exchange."

Chris added, "What about who you share it with as a measure? Many people donate to the arts rather than addressing world poverty. Should one get more credit than the other? Or what about the amount you donate compared to what you have?"

"I don't think that we need to create a complicated formula to calculate wealth, but we need to include generosity and sharing," said Ben. "The key is to provide motivation for people with excess to share with the needy and provide examples that motivate others."

"But it's true," said Alex, "that someone who gives $10 to the poor when that is all they have is more generous than someone with millions giving $1,000."

"That's true; the $10 is more generous than the $1,000."

"So, the annual list of wealthiest people could be topped by people who work to channel money to help those in need. If that were so, then years ago, we might have seen Mother Teresa at the top instead of some CEO."

"That's the thinking; it motivates people to be kind to others and to be recognized," said Ben. "My years in Human Resources have taught me that people who feel that they are doing something meaningful to help others are happier and more productive. If people found similar motivation in happiness as they do in money, everyone would be more effective. This could lead to reevaluating the pursuit of money while sacrificing family and personal time."

I added, "Just to be sure that I understand, let me summarize what I've heard. Since money makes up the foundation of our society and defines us, we need to think differently about money. There is power and influence that comes with wealth and our attitude can be one of hoarding or sharing. We can share and have resources flow back to us or we can look the other way while people starve. Since our wealth is a measure of

Chapter 9 | Money

success and satisfies our ego, this can make us reluctant to share, so we must redefine our measures to reflect happiness and kindness to others. That certainly is a new way of thinking about money. Do you see other topics that we need to discuss that will help us to think differently?"

Chris answered first. "If we eventually are going to try to create new possibilities, we will have to discuss leadership and how to make it effective. In an environment that will require a different level of thinking, there will need to be changes."

"I agree," replied Ben. "Today's leadership has not brought us any closer to resolving our problems and a discussion may help us to understand why."

"What about you, Alex?" I asked.

"I think leadership needs to be discussed, too. It's a critical element for success."

"Let's plan on discussing the leadership role and how our leaders need to think differently in the future. I'll see you on Friday."

Chapter 10

Leadership

On Friday morning I was running late because it was my turn to get bagels and coffee. When I arrived at our meeting place the wise men were already engaged in conversation. As I approached, I could sense some frustration in their tone.

"Sorry, I'm late," I said, "but I had to make the bagels this morning."

As I set up the recorder and they started on their coffee, Chris said, "I'll catch you up on our discussion about leadership so far, but, spoiler alert, we seem to be running into a brick wall. We all agree that our politicians are the key leaders since they control budgets and legislation, but they are controlled in many ways by special interests which will muddy the waters. They are tied to the status quo, and it will be difficult for them to change their thinking as a group and lead any efforts in thinking differently. Our business leaders are focused on profits and their responsibilities to shareholders. They can't be out saving the world, and our religious leaders are restrained by the separation of church and state."

Chapter 10 | Leadership

Alex added, "We all feel that these leaders have access to the resources that are needed; but for the reasons stated before they are not in a position to lead us to innovative solutions."

"What do you mean by resources?" I said.

"Resources such as budgets, legislation, problem-solving infrastructures, communication techniques, beliefs and values, and resources that are needed to study, make recommendations and attack our chronic problems"

Ben pointed out, "We seem to be discussing all of the reasons that we can't count on today's leaders to lead us into a different way of thinking rather than thinking differently ourselves. We keep falling into the trap of trying to solve the problem without changing our thinking."

"You're right, Ben, we need to look for leaders someplace else," I agreed. "Do you have any ideas?"

"My experience with empowering workers in a business environment prompts me to suggest a grassroots approach with teeth, or groups of caring thinkers operating in a problem-solving environment who develop recommendations and have some influence over the needed resources."

Chris looked at Ben and said, "How…"

"You can't ask 'how' when we are trying to change our thinking," said Ben. "We can't answer the 'how' question until we've figured that out. The 'how' will come later. Our challenge is to think differently and find alternatives to our present leadership."

"There are many good people in the trenches who are trying to make a positive difference in the world," said Alex. "If they can be organized into a force that can use their experience and insight to think differently and create possibilities, the resources that they need could be made available to them."

"People making a difference in today's world have different values from some of our traditional leaders and also are not influenced by special interests, but they may need leadership and problem-solving training in order to be effective leaders of this grassroots movement," Ben noted.

"Who are these people that you are talking about and where are they?" asked Chris.

"They are everywhere; they are the people dedicated to helping others and who are committed to making a difference as best they can. They run nonprofits, care for the homeless and operate food banks. They are professional people who donate their time to help others with their expertise. They are wealthy people who create foundations to help the poor. They are a force that needs to be organized in order to attack our chronic problems in a new way."

"I see your point, Ben," I said. "There are already people who have the mindset and the drive to make the world a better place for others. They demonstrate what we need our political leaders to do. These grassroots leaders will be the influencers who are needed to change the way we think and participate in the world. They can be the force to bring changes to our society if we can help them find the necessary resources."

Alex said, "We keep talking about values and leadership skills that are needed, but we haven't properly defined the terms. What specific traits and skills do these people need?"

Ben smiled and answered, "There is a wonderful book about leadership that has given me direction during my career, and it will help us in defining leadership and values. The book is titled *Principle-Centered Leadership,* and who do you think is the author?"

"Dr. Stephen Covey, I suppose."

"He's the one!" Ben exclaimed. "He says that for a leader to be able to think in a new way and solve deep, fundamental problems, he needs a principle-based, character-based approach that starts with himself. It's not about fixing somebody else, but about fixing yourself. Covey discusses the difference between values and principles. Values are like a map in that they help us to find our way, but principles act like a compass and show the direction that we want to go. Maps can become inaccurate as the territory changes, but a compass always reads true north, regardless of the territory. We need our leaders to have principles based on the common good and then we have true north as our goal."

"I'm a little unsure of what you are saying, Ben – can you give me an example?" asked Chris.

"My brother's street gang had values. It was important to stand up for your fellow gang members in a fight and never to abandon the gang. These were two of their values. Unfortunately, their principles were way off base. So, the map was good but where they were going was not. They had no moral compass."

"So, leaders will point us to true north, and we use our values, or map, to take us there," said Chris. "True north never changes, but our maps may change with the territory. I get it."

"A good leader also involves others," Ben added. "He needs to be a team player. Covey explains that a leader knows that he can create quality ideas himself, since he has more information and knowledge, but he also needs team commitment to implement it effectively. That will be more likely if the team is involved in creating the idea."

Alex asked, "Can't he just present the idea that is best, and they will see that and commit?"

"On a 10-point scale for effectiveness, the leader probably has a 10 idea, but low commitment since the team wasn't involved, let's say 2, so the effectiveness would be 10 x 2 = 20. If he let the team develop the idea, the idea's effectiveness might drop to 7, but the commitment might go up to 8. The effectiveness rating would be 7 x 8 = 56, or nearly three times as effective. This is just one

Chapter 10 | Leadership

example of the power that a team brings to problem solving."

Chris responded, "Finding and training leaders to take the initiative with problem solving is an important step, but this grassroots effort still needs access to resources. I see the need for some of our leaders in politics, business, and religion to see the effort and support it, especially if effective solutions are being presented."

"I agree," said Alex. "The positive approach from within will set an example and generate enthusiasm in today's leaders. If we have created new possibilities for our chronic problems, our nation's leadership can't ignore innovative solutions based on new ways of thinking."

"Well, that was another great lesson on opening our minds to a new way of thinking," I said. "Thank you all for your insight. Do we have any more topics on thinking differently, or are we ready to summarize?"

Chris said, "Any grassroots effort to recruit people, think differently, and propose possibilities will require a massive communication effort to spread the message and recruit others. Effective communication will bring people together and start us down the path to finding new possibilities. I feel that we should talk about communication."

"That's an excellent idea. We'll make that our next topic."

Chapter 11

The Message

When I arrived at our meeting spot in the park early in the morning, I was the only one there. My mind was churning with ideas from our discussions, and I was thinking that we needed to get all these random thoughts and ideas into the form of a message that could be communicated. Within a few minutes everyone had arrived, and we settled in for a productive exchange.

Chris took the lead and started with a question. "Before we can talk about communication shouldn't we have a clearly stated message that is to be communicated? We have talked about analyzing our beliefs and thinking differently which can lead to new possibilities; but I think the message needs to be more clearly stated in order to have meaning for others."

Alex enthusiastically agreed. "No one can expect to mount a grassroots effort unless the message is clear, consistent and broadly communicated. The message should be a call for people who are committed to exploring permanent solutions to

Chapter 11 | The Message

our chronic problems by addressing the underlying cause rather than the obvious symptoms. They should be passionate about leaving a positive message of hope for the future."

I said, "Let's slow down and try to put all of the thoughts and discussions into a clear statement of the process for problem solving and the type of people who can make a difference. Let's start with our objective. What are we trying to accomplish?"

Ben said, "We want to search for new solutions to our chronic social problems and instill hope for the future by thinking in a new way and studying the underlying causes."

I asked, "How do we hope to accomplish that?"

Chris responded, "By understanding that the thinking that created these problems won't help us to find the answers. We must think in a new way and create teams of individuals to develop new ideas and present them to our leadership. Teams would be trained in formal problem solving, root cause analysis and team building and how to listen."

"Who would be on these teams?" I asked.

"People who have examined their beliefs, can think in a new way, are willing to work with others on shared solutions, and are open minded," said Alex. "They would be grassroots leaders focused on the common good rather than special interests."

"Define what you mean by the common good," said Chris.

"Respecting and honoring others' needs at the same level as your own, and willing to make sacrifices for the welfare of others," Alex answered.

"Finally," I said, "how would this process work?"

Ben answered, "There would be formal groups formed with people trained in the techniques of problem solving who would make recommendations to our formal leaders who control resources such as money, infrastructure, education and communication. There would also be many informal conversation groups, like book clubs and other discussion groups, that could help us all think differently."

"So, let me summarize what I heard into a simple statement. Our objective is to create teams of people trained in thinking differently and problem solving to develop methods for addressing our chronic social problems and bringing hope to the future. These teams would focus on the common good and not special interests. Does that capture the essence of the message that we are trying to convey?" I asked.

Everyone nodded in agreement.

Chris continued, "Now that the message is clear, we need to discuss the process and the purpose of the communications. This grassroots approach will require a different type of thinking since it is not a well-funded, centralized organization.

Chapter 11 | The Message

There are presently no resources dedicated to mass communication vehicles or marketing efforts. As a first step, a target audience needs to be determined so that communications are aimed at people who can help. Methods like newsletters, books, one-on-one meetings, informal groups and social media will initially spread the word."

Ben added, "Many of the types of organizations and people that will be targeted have websites and blogs. Participating interactively can help to spread the message. The important thing to remember is to inform with a clear message and encourage the examination of beliefs and thinking differently to solve their problems. The message is everything."

Chris said, "The book that you are writing, Vince, will help to get the message out. The examples of thinking differently about important issues such as equality, spirituality, money and leadership will make for good discussion topics for the readers. Are you planning to add a section in your book for discussion topics?"

"Yes, I think that would spark some discussions among readers," I replied.

Chris added, "I said previously that we should discuss the process and purpose of communications. We have talked about the process but only touched lightly on purpose. The grassroots movement will be challenged to recruit people, solicit resources, and present recommendations without communications support. Concerned elected representatives, socially conscious business leaders, and religious leaders can all help, but the communications must be simple and clear on how they can help. Money, infrastructure and support will all be necessary in order to create an environment for problem solving and facing obstacles like special interests."

Ben added, "There also needs to be a pathway for communicating the ideas generated by teams, or what we call the possibilities. We must be able to describe the path forward from communication of the idea to how it can be implemented. Otherwise, all of these ideas will have nowhere to go."

Alex added, "I agree. Eventually our political, business and religious leaders must participate, or at least respond to the ideas put forth. But first we have to create a way to generate the ideas."

"I agree with Alex," Ben said. "I'm glad to see that we don't have any preconceived solutions heading into the discussions on possibilities. We can allow our different way of thinking to lead us to unique ideas. We all have opened our minds and are looking forward to the new thoughts and ideas that we uncover."

Chris was smiling ear to ear and just nodded. He couldn't wait for the next phase of our discussions. Alex and Ben were also full of enthusiasm.

I said, "I think we're ready to jump in and discuss possibilities. Let's all use the weekend to

Chapter 11 | The Message

generate some unique ideas for our problems and we'll see where it takes us."

"See you Monday," the three wise men responded.

PART IV

Possibilities

Chapter 12

Searching for Perfection

As I walked through the park on my way to meet the wise men, I noticed that the skies were overcast with glimpses of sun that promised a beautiful afternoon to come. It was perfect weather for a discussion on possibilities. Everyone was there when I arrived, and they were engaged in a somewhat heated discussion.

As I approached them, I said, "There doesn't seem to be much 'seeking to understand' going on here. What happened to the 'listen and respond with empathy' that Dr. Covey talks about?"

Ben smiled and responded, "There isn't much listening, understanding or empathy when it comes to a blown call by the ref in the fourth quarter of the Super Bowl."

"Now I understand. It sounds like somebody was robbed."

"You bet! I lost $100 on the Super Bowl Pool that I would have won if the right call were made. I'm going to send a bill to that ref."

"Good luck with that," I added. "I'm ready to get started on discussing possibilities and I thought that a summary of what we have discussed so far would help to get us going. Our discussions up to this point have opened our minds to a new way of thinking and that has helped us to create a process that involves others to find new possibilities for chronic problems. That path may lead us to some ideas for addressing our more difficult problems, like the hate and disrespect that leads to discrimination and inequality, or how the pursuit of money leads to hoarding and sacrifice. Other problems include the failure of leadership, the missed opportunities of global synergy and the lack of structured problem solving. This is not a complete list, but the effects of these problems on society are extensive and I hope that we can find some new possibilities."

"What is your objective for this section of your book, Vince?" Alex asked.

"My objective is not for this group to solve the problems of the world, but to provide hope in the form of new possibilities and a new way of thinking. If my readers say, 'Why not?' or even 'That won't work, but maybe this will,' then I have accomplished my objective. People need to feel that there is a path forward."

"So how do we turn our previous discussions into possibilities?" asked Chris.

"Let's talk about making a connection between the new thinking that we have already discussed and its potential effect on our chronic problems.

Chapter 12 | Searching for Perfection

I hope to show how thinking a certain way can help us to make a difference. Isn't that what we have been trying to do?" I answered.

"Where should we start?" said Alex.

"A good place to start will be some meaningful discussion on how the act of discovering our spirituality affects how we interact with others," I said.

Alex said, "Well, I can speak from experience when I say that the discovery of my spiritual self has caused me to see people differently. I found that seeking my own perfection and searching for it in others is difficult because we must look past our human behaviors. But once you can do this regularly, you see the world and its people very differently. It provides me with the opportunity to demonstrate patience, understanding and love towards others."

"But Alex, how can you ignore the crazy behaviors we see all around us and look at everyone with respect and understanding?" asked Ben.

I said, "We still have to deal with human offenses as humans where necessary, but this is about interacting with others as if you were face-to-face with God. Whether your God is the father of Jesus, Buddha, or Joe DiMaggio, how would you behave if you met on the street? You would be respectful, kind, loving and generous. I believe that is how you should act toward others when you meet on the street."

"I can see how this would have a major impact on the inequality we see all around us," said Chris. "Today we meet someone and within a few minutes we put them into a category based on their history, behavior and looks. Once in that category they suffer whatever discriminations are considered appropriate. We will behave differently toward each other if we look for the perfection and sameness."

"When we see immigrants fleeing intolerable situations, we must look through their shell which contains their life experiences and recognize that they deserve respect, understanding and help just as any other perfect being," said Ben. "We can't ignore their plight because we have considered them to be inferior. They are our equal and deserve the same things that we do. That is the attitude toward others that we are discussing, but the realities of saving the world are beyond our capabilities. Opponents of this type of thinking will argue about the impossibility of unchecked immigration on our country. They'll say that we can't help everybody."

I replied, "We aren't proposing solutions here, we are searching for a different way of thinking. Thinking the same as we always have will not help us to find solutions. There is no question that a world that is populated by people who respect and love one another will find solutions to society's problems. We would be

Chapter 12 | Searching for Perfection

naïve to think that if we saw the perfection in each other the problems would just take care of themselves. Respecting each other is just one of the elements necessary in order to make progress in our society, but it's an important one."

Alex added, "I have been trying to see the perfection in others for years and it's not easy. I learned quickly that it is important to start with yourself. You must look in the mirror and realize that you are perfect inside, just like everyone else. You must treat yourself with patience and forgiveness or you'll never be able to forgive others. Once you master seeing it in yourself and you can see through your imperfection, then you can take it into the world. Walk into a movie theater and come face-to-face with hundreds of people and realize you are surrounded by other perfect beings just like you. Sounds easy, doesn't it? Until the guy next to you talks on his phone for an hour. It becomes more difficult to see his perfection. I am looking through my human shell through his shell, and my prejudices, ego and past experiences collide with his and neither of us can see the perfection. So, we behave accordingly. Overcoming this roadblock is the difficult part."

"So, we start with ourselves," Chris said. "That puts the first step squarely in our control. We must find a new way of being instead of waiting for someone else to do something. So, how do we do that?"

Alex answered. "It started back when you examined your beliefs and values. The process of examination will help you to find who you are and whose values you are living by. When you have completed that examination, your interactions with others will change and you will find it easier to see the perfection in yourself and others."

Chris said, "Of course we can't forget the first step. We must find out what makes us who we are and how we came to believe what we believe."

"Thank you all for that lively discussion," I said. "Understanding ourselves and how we interact with others is an important foundation piece that shows how we are influenced by the world around us. Seeing each other as spiritual beings creates many possibilities. Let's move on to how money affects our lives and how thinking differently about it can lead to different possibilities."

Chapter 13

Caring and Sharing

Ben jumped in first. "Like we discussed before, money is at the core of our existence and influences us in many ways. Many people measure their self-worth by how much money they have, compared to others. Money satisfies our ego and allows us to show off with our purchases. Accumulating wealth has become the primary objective of many."

"We don't see anything wrong with an athlete being paid millions of dollars to play a game as people are dying of starvation in the world," added Chris. "There are enough resources in the world to feed everybody, but many are hoarding rather than sharing. That is the problem, motivating people to share and care."

"Money didn't always have the same control over us like it does today. Back when I was growing up in the 1960s," Alex said, "our post-war society was a place where people were focused on building their families and homes. The household budget consumed most of Dad's paycheck and everyone drove a Ford or Chevy. TV had not matured to the point where it could influence luxury purchases yet; in fact, many couldn't afford a TV. Money wasn't spent and accumulated to satisfy our egos; it was used to enjoy life. Back then professional athletes needed second jobs to carry them through the off season."

Ben responded, "So we all agree that money can be a negative influence on behaviors and many of our problems, and it continues to get worse. So how do we turn that influence into possibilities?"

"We have to find additional ways to motivate behaviors," Chris replied. "If only money is important, then it will continue to be pursued and hoarded at the expense of the poor and those in need. Our bank account feeds our sense of security as well as our ego. We previously touched on how to measure wealth in one of our previous discussions, but I don't think a specific measure is the answer. I think that happiness does not increase proportionally with wealth after a certain level. In fact, wealthy people don't necessarily seem happier than people who have enough but aren't wealthy."

Ben asked, "Are you saying that happiness should be a factor in measuring wealth?"

"Yes and no," Chris answered. "There is no way to statistically measure happiness, but in my mind, people who have money and happiness are the wealthiest."

Chapter 13 | Caring and Sharing

"How do you define happiness?" asked Ben.

Chris answered, "Happiness is sharing life with loved ones, showing generosity by caring for others, and achieving your objectives without sacrificing the other two. Ego satisfaction comes from a balanced life."

"So, by combining wealth and happiness you can also satisfy your ego," Ben said. "It seems to me that wealth that includes happiness is better than wealth that only includes money. I get it, but I still need to understand actions that connect to these new possibilities."

Alex said, "By seeking happiness through sharing and caring you can activate 'The Law of Giving' as described by Deepak Chopra in his book *The Seven Spiritual Laws of Success*. If you remember our discussion on dynamic exchange, you will recall that Chopra says that we will keep the flow of what we want coming to us by giving it to others. If we want money and happiness, we should make sure that we help others to find those things. Chopra says, 'The easiest way to get what you want is to help others get what they want.' Caring and sharing with others is an action that can connect to these new possibilities and add to your wealth and happiness."

Chris added, "We also need new role models to help us connect to new possibilities. We make heroes of the wealthy and swoon over their possessions. The media promotes the image of wealth and helps us to build the perception that wealth makes you happy and that you should collect all that you can. Luxury possessions are promoted, and people sacrifice happiness to buy them. The real heroes are caring and sharing for others and are not just building monetary wealth. They include health care workers, missions that help the needy, those who donate money to help others, and millions of others who sacrifice time, energy, money and status to make others happier. The media needs to do more to showcase these real heroes. The media is very influential in creating our role models and they can be a driving force in helping us to recognize new heroes and drive new behaviors."

"I understand what you are saying," said Ben. "We need to create a new perception of what wealth means and what it looks like. For some people, wealth includes peace of mind, freedom from financial stress, and food on the table, while for the rich it means a second home or a bigger boat. Both are probably happy since they aren't in need but is the gap the same for money as it is for happiness? Are the rich that much happier? If they can see a path where they can increase their happiness, they may be more likely to share with those in need. Recognizing this can lead to less hoarding and more sharing."

"And potentially a decrease in poverty," added Alex. "It is important that the sharing is voluntary

Chapter 13 | Caring and Sharing

and not regulated. It must come from the heart. Deepak Chopra emphasizes that intention is critical. He says that 'the intention should always be to bring happiness to the giver and receiver, because happiness is life-sustaining and therefore generates increase.' In other words, the return matches the giving when it comes from the heart, so there must be joy in the giving and then the energy will multiply."

"Great discussion," I said. "There are plenty of possibilities starting to flow today. We covered a lot of ground and outlined some specific action plans to implement some of our new way of thinking. We discussed finding perfection in ourselves and others and changing our perspective on wealth and happiness. Seeing ourselves and others as the perfection that we are and changing our perception about wealth has been stimulating to me. I still think that we need to uncover more in relation to our actions around money. We agree that new perception will drive new actions, but what are those actions?"

Ben added, "I agree. Sharing and caring are needed, but we need to discuss the act of sharing and what impact it can have on our problems."

"Great!" I said. "That will be our topic for the next session."

"Hopefully by then Chris will have received his refund from the referee and he can buy donuts and coffee," said Ben.

Chapter 14

Addressing Poverty

As I walked to the park, the sun was shining and the temperature was near 80 degrees, I couldn't help checking the weather on my phone and saw that it was overcast with wind chills hovering in the 20s back home in New Jersey. I thought to myself that I might be turning into a weather snob. As I arrived at our meeting spot, I saw Ben and Chris enjoying the sun and I said to Chris, "I don't see any donuts, is that ref not cooperating?"

"No donuts today, my friend, I thought we were all getting too fat."

"Speak for yourself," said Ben.

Just then Alex arrived, carrying a box of donuts. "I found out when I went home on Monday that I had won the pool because of that blown call, so I thought that the least I could do was bring the donuts."

"No way!" cried Chris.

Alex just smiled and laid the box on the table.

I said, "We have a beautiful day and a box of treats so now we can get started on our discussions.

Chapter 14 | Addressing Poverty

So far, our initial discussions on possibilities have encouraged us to seek the perfection and equality in ourselves and others, to look at ways of changing our perception of wealth to include happiness, and to redefine our heroes and role models. What we should talk about today is how we can use these changed perceptions and attitudes to create possibilities and how those possibilities can impact society."

Alex responded, "Our society needs to do more to address poverty throughout the world. A new perception of wealth and treating others as equals can help us to overcome the uneven distribution of wealth among the wealthy and the poor. There is enough wealth to eliminate poverty if we share resources."

Ben added, "I recently read a report on this subject, and I was surprised at one statistic that I uncovered. If all the wealth in the world was evenly distributed to all individuals, every man, woman and child would have $34,133. It helped me to understand the scope of the problem. The report also stated that most of the wealth was controlled by just a few. The top 1% of the people had 40% of the wealth and the Top 10% had 85%. I'm not suggesting that even distribution is the answer, only that there is excess wealth in the hands of a just a few."

"Poverty throughout the world is real and continues to grow," Alex added. "In my travels in third world countries during the years of my missionary work, I saw three levels of wealth. The poorest group consists of those who don't have enough and face starvation daily. Some of the people who live at this level don't have access to basic resources like clean water, proper housing and a way to provide for their family. They go to bed hungry, if they have a bed, and worry about getting through tomorrow. They live from day to day in fear."

"This level of poverty exists here in our country, not just in third world countries," Chris pointed out. "Poverty is real and can be right next door. When we have enough, we can be blind to the plight of those around us."

"You're absolutely correct," Alex said. "Many have been thrust into this level suddenly in the last year due to the COVID-19 pandemic. The middle group of wealth consists of people who have peace of mind. They have enough for now and their future looks secure, and they sleep well at night. This is the group that is shrinking and slipping into poverty. The top level includes those who have more than enough. They not only see a safe future, but they have the resources to acquire additional possessions. At the top of this level are those who have excess resources and can continue to grow their excess if they choose."

"Explain what you mean by excess," said Chris. "That seems to be where the opportunity lies for addressing poverty."

Chapter 14 | Addressing Poverty

Alex responded, "Excess is wealth that isn't increasing your happiness. Above a certain amount, wealth accumulation is simply hoarding. At this level you are far beyond peace of mind and financial security. You have provided a bright future for your family, and your needs are met. This excess that can be used to reduce poverty resides at the top of the top level where just a few control a large share of the excess."

"Aren't there a lot of people at this level who are making charitable donations now?" said Chris.

"Yes, but only a small share makes its way directly to the poor," said Alex. "Most philanthropy is directed at the arts, education, and churches rather than the poor."

Ben said, "So let me be sure I understand. The possibility that presents itself to us here is the opportunity to reduce poverty in the world. What I am hearing is three basic steps to achieve this possibility. First, we must see the need. If we consider everyone as equal and search for the perfection within each other there is no way that we allow those around us to suffer from the lack of resources if we can help it. Second, by understanding the value of happiness we can redefine what motivates us. In addition to accumulating money, we can also seek happiness through generosity, thereby increasing the flow of both through dynamic exchange. And third, those with excess have a way to share wealth in a way that brings more happiness than an even bigger bank account while helping those in need if they choose to."

"Well said, Ben," I replied. "You have captured the concept of looking for possibilities without trying to solve the problem. There are millions of details that have to be considered before a possibility such as this can be brought to fruition, but the spark of possibility will eventually turn into an explosion of ideas that lead to solutions."

"That really clarifies what we mean by possibility," Chris added. "Too often we are eager to jump right to solutions without attempting to think differently, we just follow the same path as before, which was unsuccessful. I can see how discussing possibilities instead of solutions will create innovative thinking, because solutions must be judged by others, are full of restrictions and must be proven over time. Possibilities, on the other hand, allow us to open our minds and consider things in a new way and can lead us to unique solutions."

"That discussion brought clarity on how to connect possibilities and solutions, but it just highlights the role of leadership and the importance of thinking differently," I said. "Since we need the help of our leaders in politics, business and organized religion due to the need for resources and infrastructure, we need to find possibilities for getting them involved with creating possibilities

Chapter 14 | Addressing Poverty

and connecting them to solutions. Next we should discuss how the efforts of existing grassroots organizations can influence those leaders."

Chapter 15

Leadership

"We've already had discussions on the roles of our political, business, and religious leadership and their failure to make progress on some of our chronic problems in society," I said. "But since we have focused on new ways of thinking, we see these problems in a new light, so let's search for new possibilities that may arise from a new way of thinking."

Chris spoke first. "I think we should begin with a description of the critical roles that our leaders play in addressing these problems and how they have failed to change."

"We don't want to just talk about the obstacles; it is important that we focus on the possibilities."

"I agree," said Chris, "but we also need to see what is holding us back. I think that we all agree that our political leaders control the critical resources that are needed. They have the power to reallocate budgets, create legislation, communicate a message of hope, and provide training in problem-solving techniques, to name a few. But why don't they?"

Chapter 15 | Leadership

Alex replied, "Because their principles are not aligned with true north. In our discussions about thinking differently in order to find possibilities, we've come to realize that true north means respecting others, examining our spirituality, and searching for the perfection in others. It also represents a change in the importance of money in our lives and a focus on striving for the common good. Our political leaders are following an outdated map and have lost their way."

Ben said, "Our political system makes it difficult, if not impossible, to think the way that we have been thinking. Politicians have many opposing forces driving their work. On any issue they must consider the wishes of constituents, special-interest donors, the party and private one-on-one agreements with other lawmakers. They are not able to think independently. Seeking possibilities, the way that we are, is impossible for them with all the various influences. By the time there is an agreement, the possibility is so watered down that it has no impact."

"Money and influence are the values that drive the political process," Chris said. "That is the only path to accomplishing anything; and the amount of money spent is staggering. I saw the other day an estimate of how much money was spent on the combined congressional and presidential election in 2020. I was astounded to see that the amount was over $14 billion dollars and has risen over 500% since 2000. This enormous amount comes mainly from private donors and businesses looking for influence. Just a portion of that money would go a long way in addressing poverty but is wasted by telling us bad things about opposing candidates during the election process. Meanwhile, the grassroots heroes are working their way to true north without the resources that they need. Can we create some possibilities?"

Alex said, "As we previously agreed in our discussion on communication, we need a clear picture of true north if we hope to change the thinking of our leaders. I believe that true north is where people live together with common traits that reflect their principles. The most important is equality. It is imperative to see each other as equals and, if we do, the other principles will fall into place. Other principles found in true north, like respect, forgiveness, peace of mind, spirituality, happiness, and abundance, will all help us to achieve what is good for most."

Ben said, "I agree. In order to help us to understand what true north looks like, we should consider what it isn't. True north has no categories, no hate, no hoarding, and no people who judge others. Treating each other as equals should lead to cooperation rather than competition and the drive to satisfy our ego. All these character traits are contributors to the problems that prove so difficult to solve. True north is a place where

Chapter 15 | Leadership

these problems don't exist or are being addressed by caring people."

Alex added, "To help the world understand the message, we need to highlight the efforts of the grassroots leaders who are living it day to day. Every day we see examples of people who share their efforts to help others in order to bring peace of mind and happiness. They can only do this if they see others as equals and deserving of the same things as themselves. Missionaries, churches dedicated to helping the poor, charitable donors, those supporting the homeless, health care workers and first responders. The list goes on, but these are the role models and heroes of what true north should look like. With a clear message and these role models, our political leaders need to get out their compass and plot a new direction. We need their help."

"I can't imagine that our political leaders will be able to change the influence of money on their actions," said Chris. "It's too engrained and overwhelming, even though I believe that many of those leaders would welcome a change from the status quo. Campaign finance reform is needed in order to level the playing field and provide some hope for the poor. When our leaders begin to embrace the concept of true north, they will be interested in ways to overcome the unfairness of the present system of financing campaigns. Limits on the amounts donated or a matching fund for the poor would help, but first our leaders must see the blessings of true north before creating innovative solutions to our existing problems."

"So," I said, "let me summarize what I heard. Our leadership has lost its way to true north, which contains respect, equality and change in the influence of money. The possibility that exists is that our grassroots leaders can lead by example and, with the help of campaign finance reform, drive change that can lead to additional possibilities."

"That's a good summary of our leadership problem," said Ben. "We need to support the grassroots leaders with proper resources in order to help them make a difference."

"So far we've managed to find possibilities that contribute to solving our many societal problems," I said. "At some point we need to add some structure that allows us to use these possibilities and address problems. Next time, let's build a list of problems and discuss possibilities and techniques for problem solving."

"See you then," said the three wise men as they departed.

Chapter 16

Problem Solving

As we all settled in on the next sunny Friday morning, I noticed that the wise men seemed pensive, as though they were organizing their thoughts. They seemed to be taking these discussions very seriously and I felt I had benefited by their ideas. I was afraid to ask about the referee and the donuts and since nobody else brought it up, I remained silent.

"Today I would like to take a step toward matching possibilities with problems," I said. "So far, we have found possibilities that can arise from thinking differently, acting differently and recognizing the influence that money has on society. Today I am hoping that we can look at some specific problems that these possibilities may impact. I am also hoping that we can bring some formal problem-solving techniques into the discussion in order to make them more effective for our grassroots leaders to use. First let's start with a list of some problems that our society is facing today."

Everyone jumped in at once. Chris said, "I would put discrimination, racism and injustice close to the top, followed by poverty and gun violence."

Alex added, "Abuse of the vulnerable, homelessness, and public health are problems that are chronic and need solutions. I also think that education needs to be addressed."

"Immigration, terrorism and threats to our society, such as the handling of the pandemic, are also important," said Ben.

"Well, it certainly wasn't difficult to get an extensive list quickly." I said. "I'm sure we could add many more to this list, but this will allow us to match possibilities to problems. We also talked about a problem-solving structure for making our grassroots leaders more effective in addressing some of our problems. Ben, I know you presented some structure for these discussions when we first started. Can you elaborate on how we can use these techniques on a larger scale?"

"I would be glad to share my experiences with formal problem-solving teams," Ben replied. "I believe that they may represent the most effective way for our grassroots leaders to be involved in creating innovative solutions in the future. The guidelines that we use here and that I described on your first visit, Vince, are just a part of the structure used in project teams in a business environment. Problem-solving teams are formed when a situation that adversely affects the business has become chronic and apparently unsolvable. Traditional approaches have not worked in resolving it and a team is formed to address it."

Chapter 16 | Problem Solving

"Much like the problems that we face in society," said Alex.

"Precisely," said Ben. "The team is formed from a cross section of volunteers who are interested in fixing the problem and have a vested interest and appropriate skills to contribute. Teams can include any combination of managers, workers and support staff. Rank doesn't matter since all decisions are made by consensus. The hope is that this team can uncover a course of action that wouldn't be possible without their collaboration. They follow some of the same rules that we apply here."

"So, it's not only managers that are part of the team, but workers and support staff as well," said Chris. "Each team member is treated as an equal and has a voice in the discussion. This opens the path for grassroots leaders to work with our political, business and religious leaders as equals."

Ben agreed. "It certainly does. Presently we look to our political leaders for answers when a mass shooting takes place. Congress is asked how they will address it. Why Congress? They aren't problem solvers. We need a cross section of people with passion and expertise for problem solving who can follow a structured process that may lead to solutions."

"What does that structured process look like?" asked Chris.

"In business these teams are formed in response to a problem," said Ben. "They are usually temporary and are designed to study the problem, brainstorm ideas, and make recommendations that are developed by consensus. Members collaborate by agreeing to a clear definition of the problem, searching for the root cause and brainstorming ideas that will attack the problem. The brainstorm takes place only after the problem and its root cause are defined and respectful dialogue has taken place. Listening to understand is critical at this stage."

"So the possibility that presents itself is that problem-focused teams should be the ones to recommend solutions to the leaders who have control over the necessary resources," said Alex. "By following a structured problem-solving process, they can find possible solutions to clearly defined problems. Can we come up with some examples?"

Ben said, "Gun violence is one issue that continues to plague our society. Whether it is mass killings in public places or the escalating violence on the streets; guns continue to be a source of misery. Most everyone agrees that something needs to be done, but most of the ideas run into the Second Amendment and go nowhere. The problem has not been clearly defined, so the solutions presented can never be accepted. Most solutions call for some type of ban on weapons like assault rifles or extra-capacity magazines. These types of solutions don't fix the root cause.

Chapter 16 | Problem Solving

Fewer bullets or less effective guns won't stop the killing. By bringing all sides together in respectful dialogue, where everyone understands the other's views, there is some hope of defining the problem, identifying the root cause and offering recommendation that suit everyone."

"Can you be more specific, Ben?"

"Sure" he said. "A group that respects each other and understands other views may come up with a problem definition something like this: 'The problem that we need to address is how we can prevent gun violence by making it difficult for the wrong people to gain access to weapons that kill, while protecting the rights granted by the Second Amendment.' The root cause is the people who use guns inappropriately, and why, rather than the guns they use. Obviously, there is a long way to go to solve this problem, but wouldn't it be encouraging to see all sides sitting together, listening for understanding and offering solutions that attack the root cause?"

"Now I see it," said Chris. "This approach could be taken with other problems that we discussed. The root cause of immigration that we must address is to understand why immigrants are fleeing their country and work on those issues. We also need to recognize that we need to manage immigration better in the future."

Alex added, "We have already defined some other root causes such as the relationship between categorization of people and racism."

"We also discussed how poverty can be affected by thinking differently about money and wealth," said Ben.

"A structured approach by respectful people thinking differently can certainly lead us down a new path, offering fresh ideas to old problems," said Alex. "What an exciting prospect!"

"I think it all came together there," I said. "All of the discussions on beliefs, thinking differently and possibilities tied together with a problem-solving structure that offers even more possibilities. I have one last topic for discussion. In our next session, we should discuss how we can use this type of thinking to capitalize on global synergies. If we see ourselves as one member of a global community rather than just as one nation, we will be able to find additional possibilities for addressing our chronic problems. Have a great weekend and I'll see you on Monday."

Chapter 17

Global Synergy

Over the weekend, I read through my notes and the recordings of our conversations to see if there were any other topics that we should discuss, but I concluded that taking these possibilities to the global community was an appropriate closing topic to address before we summarized what we had uncovered. As I arrived at the park, I found Alex, Ben, and Chris all there waiting for me.

"Good morning," I said. "I'm glad to see that you all made it through the weekend. Are you ready for another stimulating discussion?"

Chris answered with an enthusiastic "Yes!" He continued, "I have learned a lot about perspective and looking at things from a new vantage point. New ideas lead to new possibilities and hope for the future."

Alex and Ben were nodding their agreement.

I said, "Since we live in the world as global partners with other countries, we should search for possibilities that exist within that partnership. There are certainly more obstacles to taking a global view, but the rewards are many. Let's get started."

"We talked before about the power of synergy," said Ben, "but let's review it to be sure that we are all on the same page and understand how it works. Synergy is what happens when two or more individuals, groups or countries working together are more effective than working independently. The sum of the parts is greater than the parts added together (1+1=3 or more). It is the basic belief behind problem-solving teams that we talked about on Friday."

"I am not making the connection between global synergy and solving the problems we have been discussing," said Alex. "Countries work together now to address issues like arms control, climate change, health crises and defense alliances. They struggle getting things done due to different agendas and objectives."

Chris responded, "Synergy is never really achieved because these treaties, alliances and organizations have no teeth. All parties are not committed as equals, so that the egos of a few can result in a lack of synergy. Look at the World Health Organization and its difficulty addressing the pandemic, or the Climate Accord without all its members. For synergy to be effective, the partners must treat each other as equals and be focused on the common good."

Ben added, "To make effective use of our partnership with other countries, we have to effectively partner with each other in our own

Chapter 17 | Global Synergy

country. Success with ourselves will make us better partners and have a positive impact and allow us to generate synergy. Only then can we hope to create global possibilities."

"What possibilities are we talking about?" Alex asked.

Chris responded with emotion. "Global budgets could be redeployed for humanitarian needs by eliminating redundancies around the world, and improving worldwide response to crises. One glaring example is the uncoordinated response to the pandemic by the individual countries. We didn't learn from the initial outbreak and share approaches and information with one another, and the result was disastrous A coordinated response worldwide to public health crises would be more likely to be effective. We could eliminate the categorization of people and create a humane response to immigration worldwide. We could have trade relations that are focused on the sharing of plentiful resources rather than holding each other hostage, and we could have world scientists coming together to develop a clear definition of the environmental and climate problems and how to avoid a catastrophe."

I said, "Whoa, Chris, it seems that you had that bottled up for a while. Let's back up and discuss where you are headed with this."

"I see where he is coming from," said Ben. "Once you accept the idea that we can think differently about ourselves and each other, huge possibilities for old problems surface. We made certain assumptions in the past that may be wrong. Once we see that, a whole new set of possibilities present themselves. What if we could eliminate budget redundancies that would exist for global partnerships? There is certainly much duplication that could be eliminated in areas such as defense. Since every country feels the need for their own defense, there are duplications. If we trust our allies, then there are possibilities for eliminating duplications."

Chris added, "Countries working together and sharing resources would find ways to avoid punitive tariffs and would support addressing our environmental problems. Ben is right; once we achieve a society that is focused on the common good, many possibilities open up."

"That was a stimulating conclusion to the possibilities that arise if we learn to think differently," I said. "Your discussions have made a significant impression on me and I hope to do them justice in the book. My hope is that we can start a dialogue that recognizes the need to change our thinking. We need to follow the example of those grassroots leaders who are actively engaged in change, offer our support, and begin to ask, 'Why not?'"

"It was a learning experience for us as well," said Alex. "We've learned that our life experiences influenced us and allowed us to think differently.

Chapter 17 | Global Synergy

With mutual respect, diverse backgrounds and an unwillingness to accept the status quo, we found that we can make a difference."

"There are no solutions here," Ben added. "The problems are too engrained, but on the other hand, we can't continue to attack them with the same thinking that got us here. Solutions need to be built, step by step. New ways of thinking and exploring possibilities are the first steps."

"I agree," said Chris. "Over the course of our discussions I have learned to listen, and I have realized that I was missing a lot. I see the potential in organized, respectful dialogue."

"We have all learned from these discussions," I said. "My plan is to take a few weeks to organize my notes and recordings into a draft that you can review and edit for content. I will look you up in the park then and give you copies to review. I can't tell you how much I appreciate your inspiration. I'll see you in a few weeks."

It was good that we finished this section when we did, because storm clouds were gathering as I packed up my recorder and notebook. I watched the wise men disappear into the gathering darkness and was grateful for finding them. I never would have completed my book without meeting them. I couldn't wait to share the final version with them and hear their feedback.

Epilogue

I never saw the wise men again. I spent three weeks preparing a draft for their review and went to the park on three different days at the normal time, but saw no sign of them. We had never exchanged cell phone numbers, so I had no way to get in touch with them. At first, I was baffled. Did they head back north? Did they move to another area park to enlighten others? Did they really exist? Then I realized that their work was done, and the work that remained was just to wrap up the manuscript, which I could do alone. They had come to provide insight and perspective from their life experiences, not to write the book for me. I knew I would miss them and their inspiring conversations, but I gained a lot of hope from our discussions.

At the time I met the wise men, I was feeling hopeless. The pandemic, episodes of racial injustice, and the unchecked gun violence in the US were all affecting my outlook on the future. Ongoing chronic problems such as poverty, the destruction of our shared environment, and a

Epilogue

lack of cooperation among our leaders just added to my feelings of hopelessness. We all are waiting for others to solve the problems that plague our society, but our old way of thinking prevents us from thinking differently and creating new possibilities. We need to open our minds and change our perspective.

The wise men provided me with a gift that I cherish. Their discussions demonstrated to me that people from diverse backgrounds with a commitment to respectful dialogue and open minds can find new possibilities for old problems. Over the course of our time together, I learned a lot.

I learned that a life crisis can be a catalyst that inspires us to examine our belief system and may send us in a direction that we couldn't have perceived before. What appears to be a catastrophic event may prove to be the next piece of the puzzle in our evolution and opens our minds to a new way of thinking.

I learned that effective problem-solving begins with a diverse group of stakeholders who have clearly defined the problem and are focused on finding and addressing the root cause before they offer solutions. This leads to cooperation, understanding and possibilities that may turn into solutions.

I learned that it is easier to judge people if they are put into categories. Instead of individuals, we see groups and assume that everyone in that group behaves the same way, even though there is evidence to the contrary. We must see each other as equals and eliminate categories.

I learned that money and happiness are separate; you can have one without the other. Unneeded money doesn't bring happiness unless it is shared with others, increasing the flow of happiness throughout the world.

I learned that our real leaders have a moral compass and are always moving toward true north, where their principles never waver even when the map changes. They never lose sight of the destination.

I learned that we will never solve problems in society unless we are focused on the common good rather than special interests. Our success is measured by our contribution to that end.

I hope that you have learned as much as I have. I have tried to pass on the passion of three senior citizens who have learned to see things differently. The gift that these three gave me is an understanding that the answers lie within us and that by working together with respect, we can create possibilities and plant seeds of hope for our children and grandchildren. We don't want the present state of our society to be our legacy; we need a new way of thinking.

The Beginning.

Appendix I

Problem-Solving Process

The objective of this book is to encourage a new way of thinking that may help us to address our chronic social problems. For a problem-solving group to be effective, the participants must be willing to listen to all views, demonstrate understanding, and agree to clearly define the problem before offering solutions.

Following is a step-by-step process that can be followed in addressing any problem from chronic social problems like poverty to local issues like rising school budgets. This process will not solve the problem, but it will result in concerned people respectfully working together to use a new way of thinking to address problems.

Step 1. State the problem as we see it today.

Step 2. Have each member state their views on the problem.

Step 3. Have everyone restate the different views to the satisfaction of those who presented them.

Step 4. Using this new understanding of other views, have the group restate the problem in a way that addresses all the views.

Step 5. Have the group search for the root cause.

Step 6. Explore ideas that address the root cause.

Following is an example of the process in action. It is not intended to solve the problem or be as effective as a concerned group working together. It is merely to show how the process could work.

Step 1. State the problem.
- → Gun violence is out of control.

Step 2. State your belief.
- → We need to control the killing potential of guns by enacting laws that limit magazine capacity and the use of assault rifles.

Step 3. Listen to other beliefs.
- → Our Second Amendment rights are violated by gun control legislation.
- → It's unfair to punish all gun owners for the behavior of criminals.
- → Guns aren't the problem but the people who use them inappropriately are.
- → Gun violence is worse in the streets where illegal handguns are prevalent.

Step 4. Discuss and redefine the problem now that we understand other views.
- → People who use violence to commit a

Appendix I

crime or retaliate against others choose guns to harm others because they are available and effective. How can we limit access to weapons by these people?

Step 5. What is the root cause?

→ Guns don't cause violence, criminals and sick people do. If there were no guns these people would still be violent. They would find some other tool to inflict violence. The root cause is people who create violence.

Step 6. Explore ideas that address the root cause.

→ Problem-solving teams can now focus on the people who are causing the violence and they can mutually work on ideas that may make a difference rather than fighting each other over the Second Amendment and assault rifles.

The problem-solving process is designed to bring intelligent, caring people together to use a new way of thinking to address our problems. Listening respectfully and cooperating may change the course of our chronic issues. This book is intended to stimulate discussions, whether it be book clubs, established discussion groups or informal conversations. To view feedback and find additional discussion points, visit my website at:

www.vinceyoungauthor.com

Appendix II

Topics for Discussion

1. Name all the categories that you can be placed in. What advantages and disadvantages have you experienced because of a category that you are in?

2. Have you ever sacrificed money for happiness or happiness for money? How and why? Did you later regret it?

3. Have you or someone you know experienced a spiritual awakening as a result of a traumatic or emotional event? What change occurred? Was it long lasting?

4. I once saw a story on TV where a 17-year-old boy on the autism spectrum was staying at a friend's house. It was his first night ever away from the safety of his own bedroom at home. When he became uncomfortable in a

new situation, he would sometimes have panic attacks that took time and comforting by loved ones to eventually overcome. He found it difficult to sleep in a new place and by midnight he was in full panic attack. He gathered his stuff and left to go home to his familiar bed and family. He was wearing a hoodie and was running home when a police officer saw him and told him to halt and come to the vehicle. Being fully engaged in his panic, the boy continued to run and ignore the police officer. His hands were folded in front of him carrying his belongings, so the officer couldn't see his hands. The police officer continued to tell the boy to stop, but the boy was oblivious. This was a disaster waiting to happen. Look at this event from the police officer's viewpoint. What should he do? How could he know the real situation? What could be the effect on the boy? What role do stereotypes play in the potential outcome?

5. Why do we idolize people who have great quantities of money? Are they superior to those with less money?

Appendix II

6. You see a little girl walking down the aisle of a grocery store; she is crying, barely clothed, dirty and shoeless, and pointing at food because she is starving. What is your reaction?

   Shortly thereafter you become aware of many children in the store, all starving and in need of care. What is your reaction?

   Later you become aware that there are many more such children in need outside in the street. What is your reaction?

   Eventually they are rounded up and taken away. What is your reaction?

   How did your reaction change when the problem evolved from a poor little girl in need of food to an overwhelming number of starving little girls? Did your attitude about helping change when the problem became larger and overwhelming? Did you feel the same when the problem was out of sight?

7. Can a person be both spiritual and religious as defined in Chapter 7? How?

8. What does true north look like to you? How do we get everyone to focus on the common good?

9. Can we in the United States overcome our nationalist ego and become a better global partner? Aren't non-Americans deserving of the same things that Americans are?

10. How do you feel when you contribute to a worthy cause or a GoFundMe solicitation? Does the satisfaction you feel at helping someone else outweigh the monetary value of the gift?

Appendix III

Selected Readings

Bowman, Carol. *Children's Past Lives: How Past Life Memories Affect Your Child.* New York: Bantam Books, 1997.

Chopra, Deepak. *The Seven Spiritual Laws of Success: A Practical Guide to the Fulfillment of Your Dreams.* San Rafael, CA: Amber-Allen Publishing, 1994.

Covey, Stephen R. *The 7 Habits of Highly Successful People.* New York: Simon & Schuster, 1989.

Covey, Stephen R. *Principle-Centered Leadership.* New York: Simon & Schuster, 1991.

Covey, Stephen R. *The 3rd Alternative: Solving Life's Most Difficult Problems.* New York: Simon & Schuster, 2011.

Redfield, James. *The Celestine Vision: Living the New Spiritual Awareness.* New York: Warner Books, 1997.

Walsch, Neal Donald. *God's Message to the World: You've Got Me All Wrong.* Faber, VA: Rainbow Ridge Books, 2014.

Weiss, Brian. *Many Lives, Many Masters: The True Story of a Prominent Psychiatrist, His Young Patient, and the Past Life Therapy That Changed Both Their Lives.* New York: Simon & Schuster, 1988.

Weiss, Brian. *Messages from the Masters: Tapping into the Power of Love.* New York: Warner Books, 2000.

Williamson, Marianne. *A Return to Love: Reflections on the Principles of a Course in Miracles.* New York: HarperCollins Publishers, 1992.

Williamson, Marianne. *Healing the Soul of America: Reclaiming Our Voices as Spiritual Citizens.* New York: Touchstone, 2000.

Acknowledgments

It is impossible to recognize all the people who have influenced my thinking and helped me to arrive at where I am today. I am grateful to my in-depth exposure to the teachings of Dr. Stephen Covey and the writings of Neil Donald Walsch and their influence on my perspective. My spiritual journey was prompted by how I was treated by family, friends and colleagues after experiencing a traumatic accident. I came to appreciate the value of kindness for others that I had previously taken for granted. I began to see people differently.

Once I decided to put my thoughts into writing, I received feedback from several people like John and Valerie Coyle, who provided encouragement as well as constructive criticism that greatly influenced the outcome of the book. My sister Alice Young and I have bounced ideas back and forth for years and she has helped me to learn from the right people. My family and friends have provided motivation with their encouragement and technical support when needed.

These ideas would not be a book without the careful, patient editing of Kate Victory Hannisian and her help in making my thoughts clear on paper. My thanks to Robin Wrighton for her cover and interior design. And finally, to my wife Joan for allowing me to lock myself in my office to write.

About the Author

Vince Young began his spiritual journey 25 years ago while recovering from a traumatic accident. That journey overlapped with a business career in which he was successful in implementing the principles presented in *The 7 Habits of Highly Effective People* with coworkers. He saw the value in examining our beliefs and the use of respectful dialogue to help us develop a new way of thinking. Our hope for the future lies in our ability to understand our differences and place value in all views.

Find more information, discussion topics and book club information at:
www.vinceyoungauthor.com.

www.ingramcontent.com/pod-product-compliance
Lightning Source LLC
Chambersburg PA
CBHW022018290426
44109CB00015B/1218